Our Place

Written by Brian Moses
Illustrated by Kate Rogers

Collins Educational

Rahim likes to play in his bedroom…

but he doesn't like the view out of his window.

Esther likes to dig in the garden…

but she doesn't like the noise from the factory.

Marcia likes to go for a walk with her dad…

but they don't like the traffic fumes.

Shakira likes to shop at the street market…

but she doesn't like to be pushed and shoved.

Daniel and Lizzy like to feed the ducks…

but they don't like to see the pond full of litter.

Rupika likes to visit her Gran...

but her Gran doesn't like her to cross the busy road on her own.

Andy likes to play in the adventure playground...

but he doesn't like to see it treated badly.

This is our neighbourhood.
We think it's a very special place to live.